praise for *loving my salt-drenched bones*

Whenever pain leaves the body, it carries itself away from our skin. Triggers lessen, the mind deciphers between a war and a battle. Our bones left as relics to what was once attached and what is finite. Karo Ska became a serpent in this collection. Sloughing off the skin, trusting once again that pain is only part of this mystical process. She retells her story to her audience but essentially—she is whispering herself into wholeness. I found solace in her vulnerability sprinkled with a crudeness that comes with the beginnings of loving oneself.
—Ingrid M. Calderón-Collins

karo ska's poetry collection *loving my salt-drenched bones* journeys the honesty of staying whole despite the ache of the past, the rawness of now, and the uncertainty of the future. Ska challenges society's toxic definitions of identity and the lack of justice that exists for so many, including our dear planet. Ska's collection echoes the ancestral resilience rumbling deep within the marrow of an empowered self. *loving my salt-drenched bones* gives us the courage to open our wings of truth and take flight on a love quest to reclaim the power within ourselves.
—Alex Petunia, author of *Tending My Wild*

loving my salt-drenched bones is an examination and reclamation of body and home. a navigation of want and cost, the lost and found, the spoken and unspoken. ska paints us gracefully toward their poignant discoveries of healing, growth, and belonging.
—Sara Khayat, Manager, World Stage Press

World Stage Press
Verse from the Village

LOVING MY SALT-DRENCHED BONES

karo ska

World Stage Press
Verse from the Village

World Stage Press
Verse from the Village

loving my salt-drenched bones
Copyright © 2022 Karo Ska
ISBN: 978-1-952952-24-1

World Stage Press
First Edition, 2022

All rights reserved. No part of this publication may be reproduced, distributed, or transmitted in any form or by any means, including photocopying, recording, or other electronic or mechanical methods, without the prior written permission of the publisher, except in the case of brief quotations embodied in critical reviews and certain other noncommercial uses permitted by copyright law.

Printed in the United States of America

Cover Design by Krystle May Statler
Layout Design by Emily Anne Evans & Krystle May Statler

Rarely, if ever, are any of us healed in isolation.
Healing is an act of communion.
—bell hooks

table of contents

introduction xv
an incomplete list of techniques i use to cope xvii

scapula.
- 23 a grief i can't name
- 25 without spilling a drop
- 28 a map of my mother's pain
- 30 my mother says everyone has to learn how to swim
- 32 at urgent care with my white mother
- 34 my mother's first idea to make money in los angeles is to get me cast in a commercial
- 35 portrait of my mother as a barbie doll
- 36 an ode to other mothers
- 37 all the clouds in the atmosphere
- 38 on forgiving our mothers

clavicle.
- 43 healing isn't chronological
- 46 a poetic timeline of my complex post-traumatic stress
- 48 days like this i don't want to live
- 50 rest in peace, sleep
- 52 i dream of dying
- 53 on the gold line metro station stop
- 54 how i learned to fall in love with ants
- 56 anxiety is how my bones hunger
- 57 7 ways to say you're anxious
- 58 the jameson
- 61 i'm standing at the beach, alone

ribs.

- 65 my grandmother's cinnamon-scented arms
- 66 a voyage home
- 68 back to the past
- 70 a photo album of the places i can't call home
- 72 we find homes
- 73 a sweeter home ghazal
- 74 at dinner, my friend's mother asks me where i was born
- 75 3.5 x 2 inch hugs
- 78 after the third sunday in june
- 79 my internet father

metatarsals.

- 83 the costs of citizenship
- 85 a garden of nopales in my breath
- 86 the harmful things we say to children when we think they're not paying attention
- 88 my first day of elementary school in america
- 90 english is not my language
- 92 *but you speak english so well*
- 94 *where are you from?*
- 95 the day i spilled menstrual blood all over the bathroom floor at an alta med clinic in east los angeles
- 97 the justice of streets
- 98 waiting for rain
- 100 we fill the intersection of sunset & logan for trans day of resilience (vengeance)
- 102 fire to the prisons
- 103 i tell the land

pelvis.
- 107 my non-binary femmefesto
- 108 i don't have any dietary restrictions
- 110 rumination on menstruation
- 112 i love my body bloody
- 113 song of my womb
- 115 lessons in toxic masculinity
- 117 *no, not tonight*
- 119 i can't love like a wild animal
- 121 the blood magic of a werepussy

vertebrae.
- 125 grandma's hands
- 127 interview as a portrait of fatherly intimacy
- 129 a prayer to my ancestors
- 131 fill my bowl with a caesura salad
- 133 digging up suicide
- 135 breathe. breathe. breathe.
- 137 forget everything that came after
- 139 the charred eyeless monster in the mirror
- 141 learning to pick up the pieces
- 142 self-growth
- 143 i touch trees & feel rooted
- 144 an ode to my feathered friends
- 146 portrait of potatoes as depression
- 148 dear dawn,
- 149 a day of joy
- 150 a tulip plucked without consent
- 152 ways to be a flower

acknowledgments 155
about the author 159

LOVING MY SALT-DRENCHED BONES

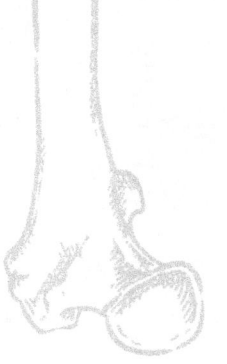

introduction

This collection is autobiographical and examines my trauma — from a mother addicted to prescription pills to a step-father's sexual abuse.

These pages are a story of my aches, my survival, and how I fell in love with myself. I hope in reading it, you'll feel less alone.

It's easy to see ourselves as leaves in the wind, unconnected, but we are intertwined. The air between the leaves is the glue holding us to one another.

My trauma is linked to larger systemic, historical structures — colonization, globalization, imperialism, cis-hetero-patriarchy, capitalism, and white supremacy. The country I live in, the united states of america, is built on a culture of european (white) violence. It is a culture of murderers and enslavers.

You and I are part of that narrative. How we resist this culture and how we assimilate into it is part of that narrative.

We can't be complacent or silent about injustice, harm, and abuse. I don't know how this current empire will fall, but it will fall.

Whenever I feel disheartened or pessimistic, I return to Arundathi Roy: "Another world is not only possible, she is on her way. On a quiet day, I can hear her breathing."

I believe that underneath the layers of pain found between the following pages, you'll hear this world breathing, too.

Dear reader, I appreciate you. You are important. You are enough. Your story also needs to be told.

content warning
The individual poems in this collection do not have content warnings. Please be aware of the following potential triggers: child sexual abuse, suicidal ideation, self-injury, depression, anxiety, post-traumatic stress, non-consensual sexual encounters, alcohol abuse, police violence, racism.

an incomplete list of techniques i use to cope

therapy.
Therapy is expensive. I found my therapist through openpath. org. You pay a one-time fee ($60) and have access to a database of therapists who will see you at a sliding cost ($40-80 per session). My book wouldn't have been possible without the guidance of my therapist. I don't think one solution works for everyone but therapy can be invaluable. If you're considering therapy, do it. I know I waited too long. Talk therapy is only one modality. Somatic therapies, such as EMDR, can be helpful if talking doesn't work for you.

support groups.
Healing happens when you authentically and deeply connect with others. Reach out to the people with whom you share similar experiences. Sometimes you need to be in a room full of survivors to really see yourself.

set boundaries.
Cut toxic people out of your life. Just because they're family or friends you've known for years doesn't mean you need to keep them in your life. If someone continually hurts you, you have no obligation to continue the relationship. Sometimes you gotta change your phone number and disappear. It's ok. You don't owe anyone anything, including your parents or caretakers.

weed.
On days, the world feels like too much, I smoke weed. Give yourself permission to do what you need to do to get through a day that's particularly difficult. Don't shame yourself for how you need to survive. You will have days that are hard. They are temporary. But don't use weed to escape your problems. Do the work on days you don't feel overwhelmed and when you need a break, take it.

meditation.
In May 2020, I started meditating every morning. A friend recommended Insight, a meditation app. I suggest checking out Lalah Delia — she has a playlist of POC meditation guides. I love her "Taking Your Power Back" track. I also really enjoy listening to binaural beats and singing bowls.

trees.
I love trees — their roots, their bark, their trunk, the way leaves sound when the wind blows. Touching trees connects me to the energies of the earth. These energies are powerful and grounding. I have a couple of tree-friends in my neighborhood I visit when I am feeling particularly unsettled.

yoga.
I started practicing yoga-influenced stretching when I was 19. Because of colonization and imperialism, the appropriation of spiritual practices is rampant. I hesitate to call my practice yoga or stretching because I think it exists somewhere in between. If you do choose to engage with yoga practices, do so mindfully and respectfully. I would caution against participating in expensive white-led yoga sessions.

walks.
Walking is great — moving your feet, seeing the landscape, being outside. But do what feels best for you, even if it's just walking around your block or your garden. Or if walking is not accessible to you, sitting outside is a good alternative.

rest.
Abandon productivity culture. Your value is not attached to how much you produce. Your value is you. Take naps. Sleep. Watch TV. Play video games. Have fun. If you need support (like someone to take care of your kids) so you can fit rest in, ask for support. It's possible that your friends without kids might appreciate spending time with your children.

write and draw.
You don't have to create masterpieces. Journal. If you're having trouble free-writing, look up journaling prompts. Doodle. Or look up how-to-draw guides. Get a coloring book or print out coloring pages online. Engage the creative side of your brain.

read for fun.
I love reading fiction, especially young adult fantasy by people of color. Some of my favorite authors include Octavia Butler, N.K. Jemisin, Sofia Samatar, Intisar Khanani, Fonda Lee, Renée Ahdieh, Roshani Chokshi, Tasha Suri.

binge-watch.
This doesn't always make me feel good. But sometimes I need to check out and not use my brain. I find that if I do this occasionally (especially when I'm stuck on a problem), it helps me relax. But just like smoking weed, don't escape forever.

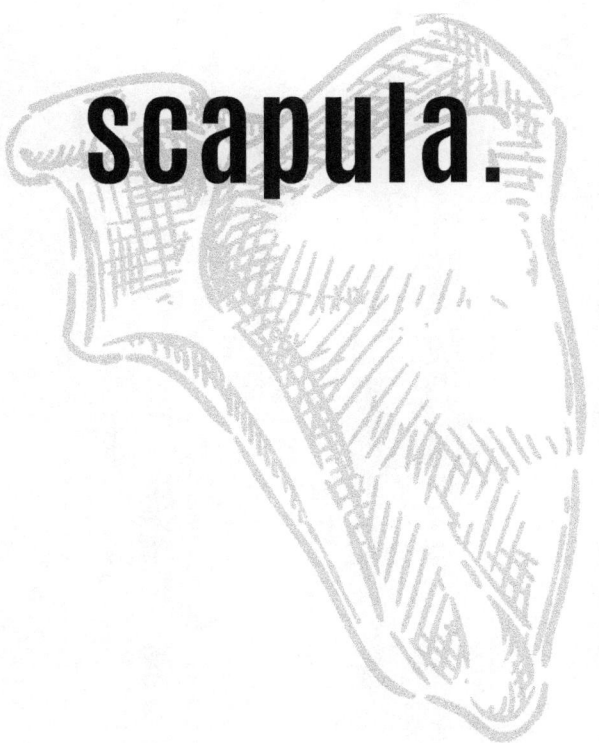

scapula.

a grief i can't name

at eight, i write my first poem
where a white & orange cat steals
my mom's baloney, runs
from the kitchen table, meat
flapping between its jaws. i keep
a notebook of silly four-line poems,
where i compare my mom
to a parrot, where i wait
for the moon to talk to me. one day,
i open my eyes & see my mom —
not a colorful bird, but
a washed-up, empty clam shell.

i'm sick, she says. the doctors don't
know why so they prescribe her
benzos, anti-depressants, tranquilizers, anti-convulsants,
until she's more pink powdered pills
than mom. i can't translate

the sounds rattling
inside my skull
into english. maybe
i'll write a poem in anguish
or in cat or in the secret
language of the moon.

how else to write about
the grief of having & not
having a mother. how else
can i find the words steeped
in pain to name the hole
in my chest where once
love grew in the giggles

of my eight-year-old self,
laughing at my mom's face
when she turned around
& saw her baloney gone.

without spilling a drop

in fifth grade, on an overnight
camping trip, a chaperon asks me

*were your parents worried
about sending you away?* i reply

my mom was. the chaperon nods
as if she understands & says, *your dad,*

he was cool with it? i don't answer,
so she chatters on, *he knew*

you'd be fine, huh? i hesitate,
not knowing how to navigate

her assumptions. finally i murmur,
i don't have a dad.

because to me he doesn't
exist. years later, in my closet

i find a letter my father
had written to my mother. i

read it & don't tell her.
in our living room, my mother plays

solitaire, arranging the cards so she
wins every time. i ask her,

*did my father ever write you
a letter?* a frown creases her

forehead. she replies, *no*, finishes
her game, walks out to the balcony

for a smoke. i taste the metallic
of her pain. i wish i could give

her a hug, but she's hugging
nicotine. & i am alone,

thinking of my father's handwriting,
the curls on his letters & why

my mother won't tell me
the truth. reading his letter, he

starts to exist, becomes real, more
real than i want him to be. i don't

miss him or love him, just wonder
what he's like, whether he

enjoys drinking coffee black or
with sugar & cream; if he has a favorite

song he listens to when he cries. for him,
to be real, i must feel his warmth

under the pulse of my thumb. our
heartbeats must share the same

breath, our dilated pupils swallowing
the other whole. my mother says she tried

writing to him, he never wrote
back. i fold his letter into the cracks

of my scapula & don't question her
lies. my mother & i, we both

carry buckets of loss, yoked
on our shoulders, we carry them

without spilling a drop.

a map of my mother's pain

my mother almost died at sixteen —
a motorcycle split her head open.
in a coma for four days,

the doctors gasped *miracle*
when she awakened. years later,
she showed off the damage — she parted

her hair & said *look, this is my scar*.
i ran my finger over her
ridge, mapping the geography

of her injury's history, wanting
to find the cartography of why
she never played with me.

it's neurological, she claimed, denying
how her sadistic mother, her alcoholic
brother, her abusive husband erased

the coordinates of her joy. my mother
healed the invisible scars her spirit bore,
with an island of volcanoes & a lava

of prescription pills, until the magma
buried her alive. i'd come home
to find her lying on the couch, an ember

without any fire. lacking friends or hobbies,
she hobbled, hollow through life's paths,
following an outdated map.

the things we deny are misguided
directions getting us lost. so here's
my truth — a nautical chart

of my mother's depression & how
nothing i did could light up her eyes.
i am the child she wished she had aborted

or given away, but how could she
relinquish what she carried for nine months
when it was in her arms, suckling

her breast? instead, she abandoned me
in pieces, her spirit dying
before my eyes. she

denied me a mother, denied me
a childhood. yet here i am, drawing
a new map, where i embrace

the cliffs of my pain & plot the coordinates
of my joy. cliffs i no longer fear
& coordinates no one will dare erase.

my mother says everyone has to learn how to swim

but i can't float. i fear the water
won't hold me. no one else has.

i lost my first kiss to a man
in his 60s. his tongue teaching

me lessons i wasn't ready
to learn. i kissed a boy

my own age at thirteen.
his mouth tasted the same —

day-old cigarettes, cheap cologne.
i drowned in his mouth, too.

if i were to define my own desire,
i'd have to confront memories i can't

recall. their fuzzy imprint leaves me
gasping. my arms flounder to keep me

above water. my mouth mimes the shape
of a fish's when it jumps out of its bowl.

post-traumatic stress is an ocean
i can't swim in without losing

my will to breathe, an ocean
where i don't have limbs

to carry me across the rip currents
of life. in my mind, i close

the dam of the flood, so i forget &
can sometimes feel normal. what is

normal when you're drenched
in a grave of your own bones?

my mother says i have to learn
how to swim, but she

never taught me how to float.

at urgent care with my white mother

she watches me check "other" under race,
squirming in the plastic hospital chair.
her eyes heat & narrow. she says,
her voice high-pitched

check "white"
 you'll be seen faster.

i taste bitter blood on my tongue.
my bones shrink, my cheeks
flush, my grip on the pen
tightens. i ignore her.

i will not allow her
to erase me. i'm white, but
i'm also south asian —
brown-hued, sand-stained. i'm
my father's child, as much as hers.

she raised me, but i see in the mirror
my mud-flavored eyes — the color
of silt where my ancestors
blossomed. a homeland i can't call
home speaks a language i hear
in the vibrations of my genes.

i could try & pass, but my bengali
grandmother says, *no*. says *be proud
of who you are*. i'll take pride
over pretending. i'm tired of making
myself fit into boxes on forms, tired
of being this idea of an ideal child.

my mother says

check "white"
  you'll be seen faster

& tears threaten my throat.
i don't want to be seen faster
by a lab coat & clipboard. i want
to be seen by her, my mother.

my mother's first idea to make money in los angeles is to get me cast in a commercial

with no car, we trekked around burbank
on foot. she held my hand, pulled
me from audition to audition, where i
would sit on men's laps while they
asked me to smile. i never did. they
never called back. i fluttered
back into my cocoon, begged
to be caterpillar, begged for
camouflage & infinite legs.

eventually we stopped
going. i was declared a failure
at nine years old. in therapy,

i list the reasons i can't forgive
this woman who birthed me,
who i sometimes call mother. in therapy,
i lift her off my diaphragm so i
remember how to breathe. grazing

my fingers across my soft, tender belly,
like a dune of sand, i dream
of having a tougher exterior —
an exoskeleton, a spine i could extract
& throw like a javelin, then maybe

it would be easier to forgive
a mother who tried
selling me to hollywood.

portrait of my mother as a barbie doll

nestled inside the detachable belly
of my barbie doll is a bouquet
of plastic limbs. i twist

pregnant barbie's arm, testing her
boundaries. i pull & pull until
her arm pops off. i try fitting
the joint back into the shoulder.

it won't stick.

i put the severed arm
into my mouth, suckle it,
tonguing the textured fingers,
biting down, admiring
how my teeth fray the plastic
of her skin. how it almost
tastes like flesh.

unsatisfied, i pluck

the head off, then cry
at the broken pieces
of a mother. i cradle
the head, brush the hair,
watching how the painted
smile never shifts, never
changes, as if dead.

an ode to other mothers

one night at bath time,
my mother tries scrubbing
the brown out of me, grating
a ridged sponge over & over until
i'm crying, my flesh
tinged pink. my nanny,
Renata,
stops her.

in private, Renata tucks me in
& whispers, *don't worry
about your mother. it's ok.
it's not your fault, she's sick.*
for years,

Renata saves me, taking me
out to feed ducks
at the pond & listening
to my toddler-talk. a mother
is not a mother

because she gives birth. a mother
is birthed
when she sees
her child not as the smallest
matryoshka doll buried
deep inside, not
an exact tinier replica, not
someone to carve. a mother
is birthed
when she sees her child
as flesh, bone, skin,
& imperfectly perfect.

all the clouds in the atmosphere

a heavy club of grief twitches
in my belly. what am i
avoiding? how many poems
have i written but never said
i haven't talked to my mother
in nine years. nine years
is almost a decade. a decade
is one tenth of a century. & i'm
almost one tenth of a daughter.

a choice to be motherless
when i'm already fatherless.
what am i avoiding, if not
how i severed the placenta
before i was birthed. which is to say
all the clouds in the atmosphere
can't fill the tears i haven't cried.

on forgiving our mothers

mom, you were not there
when i needed you.

no patience for children, no patience
to teach me how to spell or how
to add fractions. you hired

a tutor or a nanny when you could,
& when you couldn't, you left me
to wipe up the blood
from my scraped knees. mom,

i tried helping you. i tried
making it easier — i did
the dishes, i made the bed.
but you growled at me —
*a dog could do a better job
than you.* & when i told you

about my day at school, you
said, *learn to be quiet.* & when
i asked if we could go to the park,
your eyes dulled & your body
sighed, *no, i'm too tired.* you
laid on the couch like a wilted tulip,
your petals broken off. decades later,
my chest yawns unfulfilled,
missing the love of a mother.

mom, you loved me
in your own way. a way i didn't
understand. every morning, you
made me a hot cup of honey —

a golden steaming potion. you took me
shopping for new clothes & let me pick
what i wanted, even when
it wasn't on the clearance rack.
you told me i was smart. you knew
from the beginning, when you first
looked into my eyes. mom, i'm trying

to forgive you, trying to remember
how you cared for me, how you
held baby-me, how my mouth
suckled your breast. mom, i'm

trying to forgive you, trying
to heal the wounds only a mother
can inflict. i'm trying to forgive
you, but i'm not there,
not yet.

clavicle.

healing isn't chronological

1.
i cling to the rise & fall of my lungs —
anger ravaging the oceans of my mind.
i meditate every day. it's not enough
to quiet the sirens in my head. i can't

calm the category four hurricane
throbbing at my temples' port. i'm
a bay of emotions, a thunder
of irritation, lightning crackling
in my bones. metaphors & imagery

drown my truth — the words i'm too afraid
to say. salty memories haunt
my dreams — the trigger of soft skin
pressed against my face. i wake up

in panic, wanting to vomit
at the idea of touch. i've given
my body away too many times.
i need it to be mine, for now,
forever, for however long
the sirens in my head sing.

2.
once, a boy fingered me in a movie theater.
we were watching (or not watching)
the clone wars & i was a freshman
in high school. i wanted to be
loved so badly, but i hated
every minute of his finger
clumsy in my jeans. the next day,
i giggled about it because i wanted

to be normal so badly, but i hated
every boy who said hello, so i
said i was a player & never called
any of them back. in eighth grade,

i played strip poker in the handball
courts, almost got suspended, but they
said i was a *good kid*. i wanted
to be seen so badly, but i hated
all the looks & stares. my step-

father once said he never did
anything to me, & i believed him.
now i wonder if he only wanted
to make sure i kept his secret.

3.
i chased so many things
i didn't want, chased a version
of myself that wasn't me, hiding
from the truth, hiding from the memories
the ocean washed away from me.
i want so badly to make peace

with where i'm at, but i hate
how the trigger of soft skin
haunts me like a ghost storm
of my past. i cling to the rise
& fall of my lungs, i meditate
every morning, tell the sirens
in my head, *i am letting go.* sometimes

they listen. sometimes i cry. healing
isn't chronological. it's a monsoon,
seasonal & shifting, guided
by the atmospheric pressure

of my body & the temperature of
my emotions. & every day, i pray
i'll live to see the blue sky once again.

a poetic timeline of my complex post-traumatic stress

at birth, i learn death can be a breath
away when my mother's cells try
killing me upon my exit

from the womb. at three, i learn
my mother is not immortal, but epileptic
when she collapses from a seizure. at eight,

i learn my consent is not mandatory
when a step-father's mouth finds mine.

at thirteen, i fall in love with how a blade
cuts into my flesh, how blood & pain
eases the opera of my skin. at sixteen,

i learn to be disembodied, drinking
cough syrup & popping my friend's
prescription adderall. at twenty-three,

a man pushes me into a bathroom stall
at a party, the non-consensual taste
of whiskey & cigarettes on my tongue.

at thirty, when the toaster pops or when i
drop a stack of plastic spoons at work,
i yelp like a coyote hit by a car. i'm told
stop overreacting. it's annoying.

but they don't know, i can't stop
because my body is always
on high-alert. needle poised

at imminent threat. muscles coiled
like a nautilus shell. hooves pounding

in my chest. i remind myself — inhale,
kiss the diaphragm, exhale.

at thirty-four, i learn to let go,
take steps back, say, *this is
post-traumatic stress, not me.*

every morning, i repeat, *i am safe.
i am loved. i am powerful.* until,
i believe it. (most of the time.)

the coils in my neck, in my shoulders, in my jaw
loosen, one by one. day by day. year by year.

at forty-two, i am a pink petal
skimming the surface of a lake
guided by a current, buoyed
by decades of growing roots

strong enough to blossom,
strong enough to let the wind
carry me towards my dreams,
strong enough to say

i am safe

i am loved

i am powerful

& not doubt myself.

days like this i don't want to live

what are the words for *i don't feel good,* words
for *i'm triggered,* words for *my body sizzles
like a steak on a grill.* i take a shot of jameson,

calm my charred nerves. i am the cow on the train
tracks who doesn't move despite the blares
of the horn. i'm not running from my pain,

it's simply too heavy for me to carry. i want to
call it quits, stop trying to heal, drown
in my drama. i want to keep drinking until i

pass out. days like this i think about Palestine.
i think about occupation. i think about war
& the drones paid for by my taxes. i think about

Kashmir or the Indigenous people
of the Chittagong Hill Tracts, their land
submerged by the construction of an american-

funded dam. i think about the world's grief
& my own, how they intersect & how
they don't. how i migrated

to america, & how that's settler colonialism. how
i'm trying to be a solution, but sometimes i'm
the problem. i crave a connection to land i

can call my own — a land that'll welcome
me. i'm trying to heal so i'll have the strength
to fight for our liberation. i'm meditating, practicing

yoga, drinking tea (quitting coffee), breathing
intentionally. but some days, i fail & pray
to a bottle, pray for the spirits to calm my ravenous

flesh. sometimes it's the self-destructive habits
that make me feel better. i am not perfect. days
like this i don't want to live, but the ancestors

in my blood tell me it's not my time yet. they give
me a home where i'm not a piece of meat
but a bird of prey with a nest of hungry chicks.

rest in peace, sleep

on nights i can't sleep, i smell myself
rotting under the covers. fly larva
pupates under my skin, eating

my flesh. i decompose, feeding
the trees of my dreams,
urging them to grow & root

me into the unconscious where
i can bloom & shake the stench
of death from my pores. on nights

i can't sleep, i stare at the ceiling
counting my breaths, showering
my body with a golden sunlight,

soothing the fiend in my veins. on nights
i can't sleep, my sheets stick
to my internal wounds, pulling & plucking

memories. memories like towels left out
in the sun, bleached of color
& feeling. achromatic images

like dreams so i wonder whether i'm
still awake. on nights i can't sleep,
i listen to car tires crying to the concrete;

i listen to truck engines wheezing
at red lights; i listen to sirens bleeding
into the sky, wondering if this is what

death feels like, swinging between
drowsy & lucid, unable
to choose. on nights i can't sleep,

my body is a corpse, decaying
under the stars, trapped
by the gravitational pull

of the moon & the magnetic
squeeze of the earth's outer core.
then the sky shifts from cement

to blossom & i am no longer
trying to sleep, but dreaming
in waking life. my head, a cemetery

without any graves. my eyes, a tomb
leading to nowhere. my nose,
a carcass of rancid bones.

i dream of dying

i breathe into my uterus/wishing
it'd rupture/wishing i could get over
the wounded rat gnawing on my flesh
at night/i don't know who i am, except
a prayer for death/on the bathroom floor,
i cry, bloody cockroaches crawling
down my cheeks/i tell my mirror self

— i am strong —

neither of us believes it/

i have a life i don't want/how selfish of me/
a stack of laundry yells at me
from across the room/i'm unable to pick
myself up/i wallow in my sadness as if
that's gonna do shit/i want to cut my body
open, eat my organs for breakfast/feed
the leftovers to a pack of hungry rodents/
body, either die or stop hurting —
if this is what being alive means,
take it back/i don't want it/

on the gold line metro station stop

feeling hopeless?

don't feed
the birds, don't eat
or drink, don't skate —
board or bike ride,
don't loiter & don't listen
to loud music

thinking about suicide?

up to $100 fine or six
months in jail

we can help!

proof of validated
fare required

how i learned to fall in love with ants

dozens of ants crawl on my desk,
inspecting a potato chip crumb.
one climbs to the top
of my empty tea mug, hesitates
at the rim before
slipping inside. my meditation

guide says *let your thoughts
float by* — clouds or leaves in the sky.
i can't. my thoughts swarm me — ants
scurrying in my brain, clammering
for my attention. they tunnel
into my amygdala & hippocampus, building
infrastructures of worry & shame. *what am i
gonna eat for dinner? wow, i can't believe
i said that. do they hate me? i am
not good enough.* my thoughts are
scampering insects, touching
antennae — one thought leading
to the next before i remember

oh, yes, the breath. oh yes,
the diaphragm massaging
my internal organs, my big toe
inhaling. it's hard to say
bye to my thoughts — they are
my closest friends, but they aren't
me. it's hard to be present & befriend
my body. a body that's angry

at how i neglect it — forgetting to feed it
or bathe it, burying its pain with weed
& shots of tequila, hoping to poison

the ants making a home under its skin.
it quiets their scampers, slows down
their hunt for the body's aches. but
sobriety returns & i can't escape
the ant infestation on my mental health.

day by day, i tame the ants without
killing them. i practice
patience & presence. i feed them
honey & sweet affirmations–*i am powerful,
i got this, i love & accept myself*–until
they're satiated. i coax them to come
marching out on the page–acrobats forming
letters & words. i forgive the ants

for their proliferation, grateful for what they
can teach me. extermination is not
my goal. i see them, i honor their holy existence.
then

i let them go with an exhale, take a step back,

watch them scurry & explore, falling in love
with my flaws & my anxious, ant-filled brain.

anxiety is how my bones hunger

anxiety loses itself in my clavicle/air sticks in my throat/lungs choke/skin vibrates/jaw clenches/teeth grind/temples throb/eyes muscles tense/bones hunger/anxiety is

the hum in my body/an itch i scratch until my skin peels off/an expired engine/needing an oil change/i've crossed

thousands of miles/driven through glass shards & rusted nails/never stopped/now i can't move/i have nothing left to give/

i sneak a shot of tequila/from under the couch/wanting to kill the beast panting & prickling in my belly/soon i de-attach/i am a burning lake of honey/not buzzed or drunk/just no longer

present/grateful to not witness my own unraveling/my brain — sticky & thick/i watch the sun travel across the sky/drop into the horizon/waiting for the day to end/

anxiety is where my bones come to eat/when they hunger for something/other than my skin

7 ways to say you're anxious

1.
your jaw clenches, your teeth squished together
like commuters riding the rush-hour train

2.
your shoulders swallow your neck, kiss your ears —
mountains form under tectonic pressure

3.
a ghost's fingers wrap around your throat — cold
& cruel, your screams are invisible

4.
embedded in palms, the thorns of a pink
prickly pear you picked without any gloves

5.
in the mornings, dread does laps around your
skeleton, marathoning buried bones

6.
your circling thoughts are vultures or crows, they
threaten to peck out your dry-roasted eyes

7.
you're the tart after-taste of pineapple
— a juicy golden disappointment

the jameson

i wake up, thinking about how
next to the flour
in the kitchen cupboard
sits
the
Jameson.

i wake up, thinking about how
next to my mistakes
in the shelf of failures
sits
me. how i am not perfect.
(and if i am not perfect,
how can i be worthy?)

i wake up, thinking about how
the
Jameson
could dissolve these thoughts,
could erode my mind,
flatten my anxiety. it's not that i

care what other people think.
it's that the mother
in me has high expectations,
modeled after the woman
who birthed me. the woman,
who at my college graduation,
didn't say *i'm so proud of you.*
she said, *when will you
get your master's & phd?*

i don't drink
the Jameson.

i keep thinking to stop myself
from drinking, negotiating
with myself — *after
meditating if i still can't
stand the feel of my skin
then i'll take a shot*. when

the teeth under my flesh grow
longer, i re-negotiate, pretending
i'm not addicted, while
making deals with my
addiction. i pretend i don't

carry tequila around
with me in a water bottle,
taking sips while
smiling close-mouthed, hoping
no one will smell the stench
of my addiction. my desire
for the heat of spirits
presses into my blood. their heat
smothers the mother in me,
my liver grimaces.

i don't drink
the Jameson.

each day, this gnawing fades
a little bit. i tell the mother
in me to be kind. they don't
know how, so i teach them.
i hope they listen. i'm undoing
decades of self-abuse, so i'm patient
while in the kitchen cupboard,
the Jameson
trembles & coughs, lonely for me.

i don't drink
the jameson.

i pretend i'm glad at least somebody
wants my lips on their neck.

i'm standing at the beach, alone

i walk backwards through time,
looking for my eight-year-old self,
wanting to cradle & comfort her, take
her away from moments i can't
remember into the present where i am
safer. i walk backwards
through time into a room i walled off
long ago, walling off what hurt me.

my therapist says my brain
protects me, but i want to know
what he did to me. i want to know
where his hands, his mouth, his
cock went, if anywhere. only
my eight-year-old self knows.

i walk forwards through time, carrying
her to a beach where the sand
is the color of my skin & the ocean
tastes of my sweat. she won't wake up
— a limp & flaccid fish — her gills
shuttered & sticky. her eyes
— well her eyes — they're   gone.

i can't remember
what she didn't see.

i place her near the ocean's infinite tongues,
kelp in my throat, praying the water
will revive her. the waves smell her
blood & swallow her into their depths.

even her imprint is gone. i'm
standing at the beach, alone.

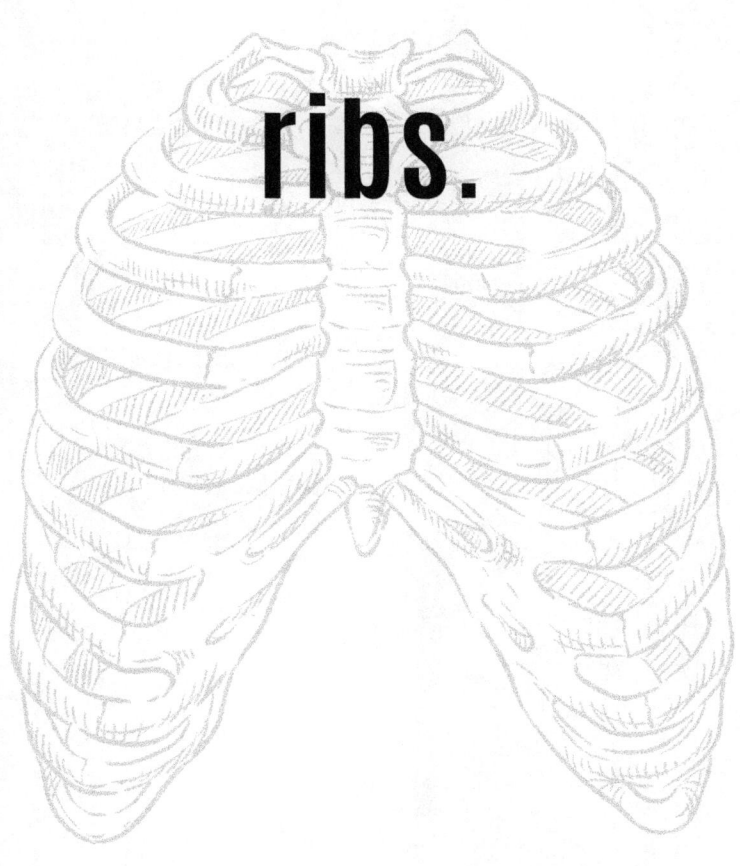

my grandmother's cinnamon-scented arms

i look at flights to bangladesh / research monsoon seasons & best times to visit / watch youtube videos of tigers in the sundarban forest / compare prices of package tours through tea plantations / peruse hotel prices in dhaka / i look at flights to bangladesh /

where my father lives / where his family lives / khulna — where he grew up / half my genes connected to land i have never seen / afraid they'll call me american /

for america stamped itself on my skin without consent / will their eyes wander through my sand-hued flesh / wondering where i'm from? /

i want to belong / i'm afraid the bengalee blood rushing in my veins is not enough / i'll be a stranger where i hoped to discover intimacy /

i look at flights to bangladesh /

budget / take notes / calculate costs / google map satellite views / ponder my savings /

my passport expires / i told myself i'd go before it did / i daydream of meeting my grandmother in a bustling city center plaza / she knows who i am / it's the eyes she says / just like your father's / she takes me to her home / where we pray / she does my hair / presents me with a sari / she doesn't say bastard or half-caste or half-breed /

i look at flights to bangladesh / i look at flights to my grandmother's cinnamon-scented arms / they cost too much /

a voyage home

in the mornings, in extended child's pose
   i repeat, *i am safe* & choke
      on my tongue — my third eye
         reaches for a home
            underneath the concrete
               mess of civility & my cracked/memories. i search
                  for home in the dictionary. its definitions evade
                 me. my roots are snakes. they hiss, spitting
              venom. i try burying
            them, but they leave twin bites
         on my wrists. for eighteen years,
            my home wasn't safe. home was
              a mother drowning herself in painkillers
               & debt. home was a microwaved dinner
                or chinese takeout. home was where
                   i took an exacto knife

        to my wrist — where the blood
        felt safer than watching
        my mother kill herself with prescription meds.

        in the mornings, in extended child's pose
        i repeat, *i am safe* & choke
        on my tongue — my third eye reaches
        for a home underneath the concrete
        mess of civility & my cracked/memories. my tears
        run like wolves down my cheeks,
        growling & yipping. i unlearn

        eighteen years of fear, one day
        at a time, third eye feeding
        from the earth, murmuring,
        i am safe. one day
        i'll believe it & befriend the snakes
        hissing in my roots. one day i'll
        make it home without
        bites on my wrist.

back to the past

in 2019, disney re-releases *the lion king* in cgi, starring beyoncé as nala.

the original hand-drawn big-screen cartoon came out in november 1994.

the weekend i went
to a dinner party
with my mother.

our first & only.

i brought a centerpiece —
a turkey i drew — my four
fingers its feathers, my thumb
its head. after dinner
the kids & adults planned
to go to the movies,
but my mother complained,
i'm tired, i'm tired, i'm tired

& took me home.

it would've been
my very first movie
in technicolor & dolby sound.

in 2019, i'm trying to re-live my childhood, trying to go back
in time, but mufasah still dies
again, again, again.

simba paws the tender slope
of his father's snout, trying
desperately to wake him.

i, too, stroked the skin of my mother,
hoping to wake her
from her drug-induced slumber.

in 2019, a tear sneaks out
through a cracked window
of my eye, my cheek
guides it toward my ear
out of sight.

four seats down someone
wipes away nostalgic sorrow — i
keep rubbing mine,
grieving for a child-
hood i never had.

a photo album of the places i can't call home

if i close my eyes, i can picture
the american embassy in costa rica
— spiraling white columns, bullet-proof
teller windows, & a door too heavy
for my seven-year-old body. i can picture

how the door laughed when i pushed
it open, smashing my toes, blood
honeying my shoe. i didn't cry. i

could smell the stress on my mother's
sweaty brow. the embassy denied her
the visa to the country she left
her home for. she hoped,
as immigrants do, for a gilded life
from sea to shining sea. for seventeen months,

we haunted costa rica, money ghosting us.
i skipped second grade, made friends
with dogs in rural villages,
who spoke the same language i did —
the subtle tilt of a head, the delicate
movement of nostrils discovering
a new scent. if i close my eyes, i can picture

lady, the german shepherd. i can smell
her fur, how her tongue roamed
my cheek, like she, too was lost
in a foreign country. if i close my eyes

i can picture the tropical gardens,

where i spider crawled over an anthill,
slipped, collapsed their home
with my butt. they, too, were angry
at how quickly home disappears.

if i close my eyes, i can picture
the winding staircase
of my first home & the soft palm
of my mother's hand, the night we fled.

how quickly home disappears
replaced by embassies & bloody shoes.
if i close my eyes, i can picture
the los angeles skyline flitting across
the night sky — a horde of giant fireflies,

but what i can't picture
is the smile on my mother's face
when we landed at lax or whether she
held me that first night we slept
in the city i now call home.

we find homes

a finch flies into a bronze
three-dimensional *n* mounted
on the side of a school, disappears

into her nest hidden in the cracks
of cement. don't we find homes
where we can? searching

for safety away from hawks & coyotes
trying to eat what we cannot
protect. for isn't home a place for us

to be ourselves & not fear the predators
lurking, suckling our pores, living
under our skin? we find homes

where we can, in the cracks
of our egos, shrinking our bodies
to fit a pre-fixed model of who

we think we should be. knowing we
must confront what consumes
us at night & not run away

from sharp teeth. sometimes we
must abandon the idea of home,
build a nest out in the open, & believe

we'll survive despite the odds.

a sweeter home ghazal

wish i could tell you how i left a tender home-
land, flew across an ocean to a grander home-

stead. i tell you i shifted from a hollow nest,
flew through the cracked seeds of a coriander home-

sickness, the citrus taste of cilantro seeping
onto my tongue, erasing any other home-

liness. i tried fitting in, tried finding soft sticks
& bigger branches, tried building a ladder home-

ward. i forgot my wings' strength, until i released
my desire for the heartland of a mother. home-

bound, i dove through feathers, seeking a refuge with-
out fear as the guiding force. i define where home

could be. my salt-drenched bones breathe & i render home-
coming in my flesh, welcoming a sweeter home.

at dinner, my friend's mother asks me where i was born

i reply, *poland*, & she says, *do you want to go back*
to *see your cousins, aunts, grandparents?*
i shake my head no — *my family wants nothing*

to do with me. an awkward silence follows,
a silence i'm too familiar with. i tell her,
i want to travel to bangladesh where my father

lives. she pauses, blinks & responds, *i thought*
you looked egyptian. now i blink, thinking she
mis-heard me, but then she repeats, *bangladesh*,

rolling the name around in her mouth
like a foreign object. i mutter something
about india, tibet, & pakistan — none of it coherent.

my friend returns from the bathroom,
the conversation shifts. no one hears
the vacant howl of my heart. inside me,

in my chest, the cut-out shapes
of cousin, aunt, grandmother. shadowed
& hollow. inside me, two halves, that don't

make me whole. inside me, a loneliness
i'm too familiar with.

3.5 x 2 inch hugs

i learn my father's name
    from a 3.5 x 2 inch business card.
        i learn he's a film director, living
            in dhaka, bangladesh.

i want to k n o w
    more, but i can't ask.
        my mother's irises
            p   e l
             i   e
              n h
              w
            in pain. instead i type his name
                    into a search bar.

my eyes & fingers
    t r e m b l e. i discover
        my father —
            a documentary filmmaker.

i stare at his picture trying
    to see similarities. i watch him
        in videos. like me, his hands
            are f   i
                i   l e
                r f   s
                  e
                as he talks. my mother
                    says my face reminds
                    her of him
                        above the nose.

i email him —
    i am your   d a u g h t e r.

he has no idea
    i   e x i s t.

he shoots movies, travels
    from bangladesh
        to india, replies
            when he can. i ask
                to see him, he says,

not yet.

in my youthful dreams, he
    was a knight / he arrived
        to rescue me / in my adult
            reality / he is a man.

in my adult reality fathers do not hatch
    from business cards
        ready to give
            3.5 x 2 inch hugs.
                fathers cause
                    purple&black bruises.
                fathers drain
                    their spouses' bank accounts
                        for beer&cocaine. maybe
                      i'm lucky
                      mine can only hurt me
                      through the web.

      i walk away from my internet
    father. i wish i could say
i never look back.

fifteen years go by. i still search
                              for him.

are some things better seen
     from afar? his business card,
          i can't find. did i throw it away?
                why can't i remember? like him
                     it slips
                          through memory's crevices.

my fingers brush his cheek, touch
   only pixels on a screen.

after the third sunday in june

a car honks on a tuesday in june. honks
again, twice in short succession. the door
to a pastel green one-story house
opens. two boys cocooned in black,
hoodies hiding ears, emerge. from their
pockets, earphones dangle. their unsure

gait as they unlatch the front gate
mirrors their father's face.

it's tuesday, two days after
father's day. where will they
go? dino's burgers down
the street? — where they will
scarf down fried potato strips
& ground cow patties — or
will they go to a dodger game?
— where they will mumble but
not speak, cheer but not talk.

the car door slams. they're gone
& i am left looking out the window,
longing to be a fly or a beetle
riding on their windshield,
to see where they go,
what they do,
how & if they hug.

my internet father

google alerts me — *on saturday,*
your father will be
at the colombo film festival
in sri lanka. if i go,

if he sees me,
would he know? i hope
my eyes remind him
of his mother.

metatarsals.

the costs of citizenship

i rarely talk about how i migrated. how once
deportation was an unspoken shadow lurking
in unnamed corners. eight years of paper-
work, interviews, & long waits
at immigration offices chipping away
at my mother's face. she married

a monster for his social security
but couldn't stay safe living with him.
not after the night he forced his fingers
inside her while she slept. not after he
emptied out her bank account, so she
had no choice but to stay longer.

we waited seventeen months
for him in costa rica, waiting
for him to apply for our
american visas, waiting for him.
he never applied.

my mother & i trekked across dusty freeways
on foot, found a christian church, where
two white women cried a river for us —
a white woman with a bi-racial child.

the river carried us across
the american border, was supposed to
take us to lake michigan in chicago, but

my mother decided she'd rather depend
on a man, despite his lies. she took
his last name, a name whose roots
trace back to the 1800s louisiana slavers.

we came on a plane, i was wide-
eyed, bathing in the american
dream before it shriveled
into the better-known american
nightmare, draining my heart
of the love i thought i deserved.

two decades later, i bear
the scars still, think of taking
my own life when i am flooded
by the memory of the monster's
tongue in my mouth, his fingers
on my thigh. he haunts
my dreams, reminding me
of what i sacrificed to say
i am a citizen. i didn't celebrate

my mother coming home
with the documents declaring
her legal. i breathed
a sigh of relief, waited
for the divorce papers, happy
i no longer had to worry
about him knocking
on our door or his hands
reaching for my
not-yet-citizen body.

a garden of nopales in my breath

my lungs inhale cactus thorns / a garden
of nopales in my breath / shame simmers
in my flesh / scorching my neck & shoulders /
an anger bakes in between my heart
& solar plexus / i can't sleep / afraid
to dream / numb & shadowed / i hide under
a thick, polyester blanket / thinking about
the man who molested me at the age of eight /
thinking about whether he's still alive / whether
he lives at the address listed for him
in the white pages / whether i can drive
to his home / confront him with a garden
of nopales on my breath / i shed my skin
of shame through the vengeance of my
imagination / an anger shifts into thorns /
the thorns shift into words / a garden of self-
love blooms in my flesh / a bright
pink prickly pear beating in my chest /

the harmful things we say to children when we think they're not paying attention

she'll be pretty
when she loses
that baby fat,

a neighbor comments,
not knowing i am
sitting on the staircase,
listening. at dinner,

i pretend to eat
my mother's breaded
pork chops, slipping
slivers of meat
from the plate
to a napkin. later,

stomach snarling, i nibble
on a gas-station danish.
my mother says

suck in your tummy.
i try but i am left
gasping
for breath.

you'll learn, she
reassures me. she hates

i wear baggy jeans
but criticizes
the thigh-fat & hip hills
my size six shorts
squeeze out. after steaming

showers, i pinch
the skin under
my belly button
thinking

*she'll be pretty
when she loses
that baby fat.*

my first day of elementary school in america

my heart is a crab claw snapping, my palms
are sweaty clams. i'm too short to see
over the front desk of the admissions office.
the adults talk above me & decide which ocean
of american freedom i'll swim in. they lead me
down a hall to a room of desks arranged

in blocks of four. i enter & heads swivel,
curious gazes probe. a bugle trumpets
through the loudspeakers, my eyes flit
back & forth. a child points to a flag
& the words on a laminated placard
that say, *i pledge allegiance...* everyone
puts their hands on their hearts, & i
mimic them, my lips moving, my tongue
in a lobster trap of one nation, under god.

at lunch, they give me a yellow ticket
& i receive a slice of pizza
on a styrofoam plate. they won't
let me leave the cafeteria until i finish,
but no matter how hard i try, i can't
choke down the melting pot
of white cheese. in tears,

i sit at the table, staring
at my half-eaten american freedom.
when the bell rings, they frown,
say i'm ungrateful for what i am given
when others like me starve, but
none of this translates. all i know is
the food in this country makes me
vomit. at the end of the day,

i've learned i'm just another immigrant,
fish-hooked & gutted, prepared
for the empire's capitalist consumption.

english is not my language

my primordial language
abandons
my tongue. in my brain
words i knew
for eight years   disappear.

i ache   craving syllables & sounds
no longer familiar.
an empty vocabulary hisses
at the back of my throat. the snake
in my mouth   struggles
learning a new dance.   it tries
to uncoil   trips on
teef until they
teach it to say teeth
in speech ferapy.   i read
out loud   the students laugh.

english is not my language.

i search for a/my voice
within a prickly ficket.   the fistles
discourage me.   my words bleed
red on english papers.   passive
verbs   run-on
sentences   low verbal
standardized test scores whisper
*english is your second
language* / rejection
from creative writing
classes murmur *give up.*

english is not my language.

i learn to switch from karolina
to caroline. as if
an english-sounding name can
[   ] it doesn't / i learn to switch
from mama to mom   watching
the simpsons   choking
on homer-chokes-bart
amerikan culture. i learn
to use the semi-colon; i learn
to activate my verbs.

what was mine
is gone   only
   a caged
      snake remains   rattling

fangs poised   snarling

english does not language me.

but you speak english so well

i learned english too late,
my mother laments,

ashamed of her
broken english. ashamed
at the supermarket

when the cashier frowns
not understanding
her dented words.

ashamed at the hospital
when the nurse asks
if she wants an interpreter.

i swallow & choke
on shame. tongue — a clumsy
worm, struggling, shrinking
in the sun, looking for its dirt home.

elementary school kids laughing —
you talk funny.

i can't say *pasta* — the *a*,
a caterpillar with too many legs.

so i assimilate. i harness
the non-english slug writhing
between my jaws, teaching
it well, until it obeys
american syllables & everyone says
*you weren't born here? but you
speak english so well.*

my mother wrestled my native tongue
out of me — *no child of mine
will have an accent.*

at eight years, i learned english,
learned it so well as to be
unrecognizable. i look in the mirror,

& open my mouth, dirt
spills out — a barren field
of internalized shame, murmuring,
but you speak english so well.

where are you from?

> i'm from los angeles

what about your parents?

> my mother is from poland

do you have family there?

> yes

do you visit them?

> never

do you speak polish?

> no

why not?

> america snatched my native tongue out of my mouth

what about your father?

> he's from bangladesh

where is that?

> it used to be east pakistan

pakistan? isn't that where the terrorists live?

> the only terrorists i know are in america

why are you so angry? it was just a joke

the day i spilled menstrual blood all over the bathroom floor at an alta med clinic in east los angeles
for anyone killed by state violence and/or imperialism

i pull out my menstrual cup. slippery
in my fingers, it collapses
from the weight of my womb.

    SPLAT.

the teal tiles below embrace
the viscous, watery clumps. the teal tiles
welcome red cells twined together
like primordial fish or thick tadpoles. blood

scurries down my thighs, a vermilion
creek of wounded wisdom
painted on the floor
like a jackson pollock painting
or a rorschach test. what do i see —
a moth? a butterfly? my grandmother's
face? the egg that made me

was in my grandmother's womb
in my mother's baby body. the grandmother
who would later tell my mother,
i have no daughter.

before i was born, i was part
of their flesh. now all of our fleshes lay
exposed. i collapse from the weight
of my womb, wiping our intergenerational
trauma from the bathroom floor. if only
it were so easy. my therapist asks me where

i carry my mother's & my grandmother's
racism, where their disdain
for indians & muslims hides in my body —
a self-hate burrowing under my skin. i rub

crimson from crevices between the tiles,
thinking how my father survived
operation searchlight, wasn't executed
by the pakistani army. in the leftover
rivulets of blood, i see people
murdered in the buriganga river,
their bodies left to float
downstream, one by one. i scrub & scrub,
but i can't erase history. see history

written in the blood spilled on Breonna
Taylor's pillow. the blood on the six bullets
dug deep in Breonna's body. the blood
splashed on the headline, the blood on
the judge who didn't convict anyone
for her murder. i collapse from weight
of my womb. i see history in the hot blood
marching in the streets, chanting
their/her/his name. i'm standing

in the bathroom at a clinic in east
los angeles, staring at tiles, hoping
i haven't missed any spots. it's taken me
ten minutes to wipe up my blood,
that's more time than it took
George Floyd to be killed by a cop's knee.

i collapse from the weight of my womb.
the blood of imperialism streaked
across my face, crusted
under my fingernails.

the justice of streets

we stand in a circle, bathing
in the sun's heat, sweat swimming

on our faces, smiles skimming
our lips. in a circle, we stand

in an intersection, blocking
traffic, contemplating tactics.

cars honk at us. we link hands, lift
our voices to the clouds, speak with

Assata Shakur. *we have nothing to lose*
but our chains. nothing to lose. our

chains. we have nothing but our chains.
nothing to lose. we have nothing to lose

but our chains. a triple crescendo — a fire
in our throats, bellowing across streets.

we march, leaving behind broken windows,
shattered atms, scattered graffiti, burning

trash cans. they reveal our defiance. tomorrow
the papers will call us agitators. today,

we are a family. a circle of strangers bound
by our love for justice — a justice

no court or vote can give us. a justice
only our feet on city streets can provide.

waiting for rain
for Breonna Taylor & Kurt Andras Reinhold

i am dry / dry like the summers
of los angeles / dry like the dandelions

scorched by the relentless sun / dry
like the tears i didn't shed /

couldn't shed / when Breonna
Taylor's killers weren't convicted /

dry like her body / hydrated
by the flames in the streets / dry

like my anger / tinder for a fire
in my heart / in san clemente cops

murder Kurt Andras Reinhold
for jaywalking / i am lost

in the dry of my lips / in the disappeared
saliva of my helplessness / dry

like my hope / dry like my prayers /
what is there to do but to keep

speaking / keep writing / keep
being the water we so badly need /

no election will bring the dead
back to life / no politician will

stitch the wounds of america /
no judge will deliver the wings

of justice to the graves / i am
dry / dry like the promises

of democracy / dry like
people's tongues craving

a drop of equality in a desert
where the oasis is a mirage /

where they tell us they won't
use excessive force / but

the headlines don't change /
the murders don't stop /

a 500-year-old nameless genocide
dehydrating our souls / we are

husks of our potential / my belly
thunders / my feet strike / signaling

the approach of rain / in the distance /
a powerful storm brews / in the future /

a brutal empire drowns /

we fill intersection of sunset & logan for trans day of resilience (vengeance)

four lanes of punk rock, determination & joy.
    we redirect cars & buses, disrupting the flow
        of amerobotic life. where concerts must be

permitted, sanctioned, controlled. where spontaneity
    weeps under a ream of documents asking you —
        sign here, initial there, pay a fee, sign here.

a confused passer-by asks me, *what is happening?*
    is this impromptu? to which i reply, *it's organized*
        (but organized without the authorities' oversight).

i dance in the streets of echo park, twisting
    my hips, bobbing my head. the cops stand, arms crossed,
        fingers twitching for their guns or batons. under the glow

of the crescent moon, its light refracted by the misty clouds,
    we shake our bodies to the rhythm of gender rebellion, to the songs
        of Black trans uprising, to the drums of liberation. at the end,

we form a circle & chant Assata into the stars above. i hope she hears us in cuba. people look on from their balconies, curious or scared. someone reads a poem. i cry, the words cascading over my body like salt water from a healing spring.

fire to the prisons

light a match in honor of car thieves / pour out gasoline in honor of self-defense / blow on the flames in honor of the incarcerated 19-year-old / he does six years / gets out for six months / back in to do four more / his sister waits then waits / again / fire to the prisons! fire to the shame! *i'm not a bad person* splutters from formerly caged tender lips / fire to carceral culture! fiiiiire / fiiiiire / fiiiiire / fiiiiire / until from the ashes / resurrected birds of orange & blue arise / their talons

i tell the land

you deserve better. you deserve more than
leaky pipelines crisscrossing your heart,
nuclear reactors spewing atomic waste

into your lungs, pesticides seeping into
your skin. you deserve more than a species
who thinks they need money more than you.

every month, i pay rent & enable
your theft. i dream of co-ops & no-cost
housing, of vegetable gardens & open-air

free markets. dear land, how do we
evict an empire? how do we fight
guns with words & bricks? how

do we recover your magic our bulldozers,
gmo's & aerosols destroyed?
i keep writing, searching

for the incantation to set you free.
i tell you, i need more time, but
time is running out at the speed

of glaciers melting. i press my palms
into your dirt, splaying my fingers, a holy
invocation — a prayer. i tell you, i see

your future. a future of ready-to-pluck
berries, their juices painted on the lips
of the people who dared to dream

of a land without dollar signs.
you breathe. a wind frollicks
in the tresses of my hair, a leaf

taps my shoulder, rain kisses me.
me & you, we are alive. & we
deserve more.

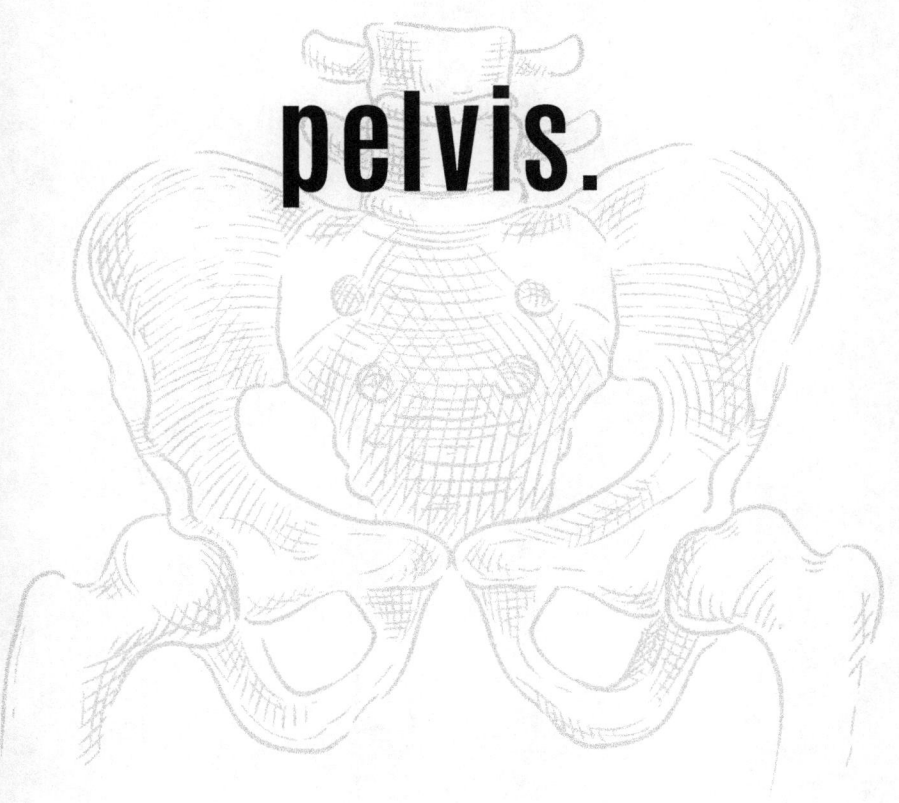

pelvis.

my non-binary femmefesto

i am afraid that when i write a poem
about my womb, about how it bleeds
every 28 days, you'll think i'm a woman.

short skirts, leg hair, menstruation
don't define me. my vagina & clit
are body parts — wet & hungry gifts

from the universe. they are constellations
inside my flesh. remember that our fates
are our own interpretations of the future,

not a blueprint of our possibilities. i am
gender fluid — a river reflecting
the multiplicity of stars. honoring my truth

means honoring my femininity
as not-woman. my gender is not
a definition, not a letter on my birth

certificate, not someone's opinion
or decision. my gender is how i
vanquish cis-galaxies & femmefest

a universe of infinite identities.

i don't have any dietary restrictions

like my sexuality, my diet knows
no boundaries, changing
daily, weekly, monthly, yearly.

some days, i gnaw on chicken breast.
other days, my tongue wraps
itself around asparagus or celery.

today i order un taco de papa. tomorrow,
i'll have your lengua, flesh
melting in my mouth. why settle

for sliced wonder bread when i
could have focaccia or brioche
or a still warm bolillo from the panaderia

down the street? i like my lovers steaming
in my fingers. i want to unfold them,
savor their softness, their buttered dough.

desires like apple varieties from gala
to red delicious or pink lady. some days
i'm vegetarian. other days,

especially when the moon is full,
i devour carne asada burritos,
licking fatty oil from my palms.

most days, i trace my fingers along
my red spotted mango,
undecided but joyful. i am

my own sweetest fruit, my own
honeyed pleasure, not needing
anyone else's flavor.

rumination on menstruation

inside me, strawberry jam
thickens
before leaking, dripping

then gushing. an 11-day-early knock
at my cervix door. the moon
& me unsynced.

the moon — predictable, well-
behaved. not me. not
this month. does my flesh crave

reproduction? is it angry
i won't host a family
of cells? i have

no home, no land i can call
my own. i can't grow
children without roots.

i can't grow glass
inside my skin. i flush
ragged parts of me, refusing

my darwinian legacy. what is
success of species
in a world of children

caged or children
shot or children
starved? what is success

if not burgundy blood, flowing
down my leg, screaming,
i'm alive? what is blood

without a wound? a womb
without a child or words stamped
with ink on the flesh of trees.

i love my body bloody

every 28 days, my uterus rises
golden burgundy & rayed clots
run down my legs —
thick, dark, brave.

i shed. i am more spider
than woman. an arachnid
molting monthly. i am more
tulip than human, blooming

from the earth, hungry & craving
the smell of my cunt. every 28 days,
i love my body bloody — urgent, insistent, over-
flowing. i am red zebra

stripes painted on my thighs,
dripping onto my new
bathroom floor mat. i am
the crisp crimson stains

on the bed sheets, soaking
into the mattress — a permanent
testament to how i am
abstract art of oxidized brown

splotches. i am the sanguine
sun, spiraling into hemispheric
regeneration. every 28 days,
i love my body bloody, flinging

vermilion flecks into the sky,
celebrating my menstrual meteor
shower bleeding across
the eternal night, every 28 days.

song of my womb

[chorus]
i enter my womb. it is dark,
wet, & warm. it feeds me a cornucopia
of pistils, pollen & nectar.
i am its honey bee.

[verse 1]
preparing for the egg, it wears
a red tuxedo adorned with
luscious, nutritious taffeta-tissue.
i angle my head up to its heaven,

[verse 2]
greeting the holy twin moons of its fallopian
tubes. inside one moon,
a lotus flower
floating out of the sky into a bloody lake.

[chorus]
i enter my womb. it is dark,
wet, & warm. it feeds me a cornucopia
of pistils, pollen & nectar.
i am its honey bee.

[bridge]
i angle my head up to its heaven,
basking in the moons' maroon glow.
i am home, i inhale, *i am home.*

[chorus]
i enter my womb. it is dark,
wet, & warm. it feeds me a cornucopia
of pistils, pollen & nectar.
i am its honey bee.

[verse 3]
i enter my womb. *i am home*, i exhale,
i am home. my breath hums a lullaby
to the moons of my womb. i am home,
home in my body.

[chorus]
i enter my womb. it is dark,
wet, & warm. it feeds me a cornucopia
of pistils, pollen & nectar.
i am its honey bee.

i am
home. home
in my body.

lessons in toxic masculinity

a boy beats the face
of a cliff near the beach.

bang! bang! bang!

sand trickles with each hit
of his stick. he chips
away at the Earth's flesh.

no one stops him.

i wince at each thud,
wishing i could yell,

don't teach him this is okay!
because what is the difference
between my flesh & the Earth's?

i trace my finger along the cliff,
gentle, soothing the Earth. his bangs
increase in strength & sound,
until he strikes the rock so hard,
the Earth roars back. the stick
bounces out of his hands
onto the ground. he runs,
grabs it, & continues clobbering.

bang! bang! bang!

ignoring him, the boy's family
walks away, laughing
at something he's too young
to understand. clutching his stick,
he scrambles after them. i wonder

what sound his wife will make
when he raises his fists to her flesh.

no, not tonight

each week at the open mic,
i admire him from afar. tonight
for the first time, he notices me.

tonight, we're both drunk,
& i am glad he gives me
a ride home. we pull up

in front of my house. he puts
a hand on my thigh, asks, *can i come in?*
no, not tonight, i reply. the next day,
he texts, *wanna meet up for drinks?*

at the jazz lounge, we both order jameson
on the rocks. his a double. i sip
slowly, reminding myself not to get
drunk. we chat about poetry, astrology,

then he leans in, his tongue speaking
unheard words into my collarbone, my
cheek, my neck. he drives me home

after a walk through downtown
& asks, *can i come in?* i reply, *no,*
not tonight. the next morning,

we make plans for later that week
to meet up at a rooftop bar.

in the elevator, he says hello
by sliding his fingers up my shirt,
nuzzling my nipples. after he spends
a c-note on drinks, he suggests,
come over to my place? i don't want to

keep spending money or drinking,
so i respond, *okay, can we watch
a movie?* at his house he pushes me

on to the bed, crawls on top of me, takes off
my shirt, doesn't ask any more questions.
my reply, *no, not tonight,* lost
in his impatient hands & mouth.

i can't love like a wild animal

once i was a lion prowling
savannahs, seeking prey.
what was love if not teeth
piercing skin, digging into
soft tissue, slurping up blood. once,

i was a starving seal swimming
under melting ice, ready to eat
anything that floated by. once a friend
asked me if he could give me a massage,
& i said, *ok*. & it turned into more.
& i didn't know how to say
stop.

once i was a turtle without a shell,
all flesh, no heart, & i was left
in the sun to dry out, & i knew
i couldn't love

like a wild animal anymore. couldn't
wake up on couches after drunken
poker nights in the arms of men,
who ate my lips for breakfast
without consent. hunt by hunt,

i discovered the wildness of my howl
& how it didn't have to be
a call for a mate. claw by claw, fur
patch by fur patch, i grew not less
feral, but less fearful of the beast
roaming the woods of my bones.

now i crave burrowed connections
& a hole in the ground i can call
my own — a self-love not built
on the brutal urges of men.

the blood magic of a werepussy

my pussy is a werecat. its hairy mouth salivates
for the taste of a full-body orgasm. it growls
in warning, spits & howls in pleasure.

during a full moon, it transforms,
bloody & wailing. during a quarter moon,
when you part the fur, you'll find it

wet & vulnerable, ready to devour
fingers, aching for a stroke under its chin.
when the moon is an unseen shadow,

the werecat is happiest alone, stalking
rabbits. it loves bunny whiskers, bunny
noses. all vibration, no thrust, just how

the werecat likes. it's been told to shave
by men who don't believe in werecats. men
want hairless cats, tame & giving. my pussy

is a werecat. my pussy is a werecat. the legends
have it wrong. a werecat is not always
feminine. the werecat belongs to no gender,

rejects any rules of the binary. it grows teeth
& smashes the patriarchy, leaving no bones
behind, refusing to give anything

away for free. if you can't make it howl,
leave it the fuck alone. it's got a forest
full of toys to keep it satiated. the werecat

doesn't hunger for men. the legends
have it wrong. men hunger
for the werecat. they're too afraid

to admit they want hair in their teeth,
puncture wounds on their belly,
claw marks down their spine. they want

the wild, but the werecat doesn't come
for anyone. you gotta be special. my pussy
is a werecat & it won't take any shit.

my pussy is a werecat. the legends have it wrong.
it prowls the nights searching not for a kill,
but another werecat to make it purr.

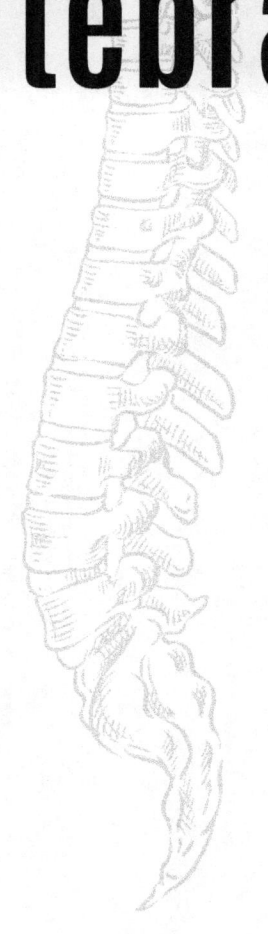
vertebrae.

grandma's hands

for the first twelve years
of my life, my mother said —
you're 75% polish, 25% indian.
who was i

to not believe her? but she lied,
manipulated the numbers in her desire
for me to be white, announcing *you
were raised in poland*, as if this changed

my genetic fragments. today i order
a lab-analyzed version of the truth.
i want scientific percentages. i want
to know who painted the hieroglyphics

in my veins. was i switched
at birth? did my mother lie
about my father's name? whose
genes do i carry in my lonely

heart-helix? can they send me
grandma's gentle hands
through the mail? my father says
to be bengalee you must speak

the language. i am not
bengalee. i am not amerikan or
polish. i wish i was 100%

intentional. instead i am
48% south asian, 48% eastern
european & 4% indus valley.
100% obscure, no links to ancestry
dot com's genetic communities.

they deny me
a family, too, give me
distant european cousins. i don't claim

national-border identities. a river
flows from a plateau, spills
into a sea, connects

to an ocean, trembles
at my l.a. river's edge. i touch
the water, i feel a pull.
maybe i'm reaching,

but i can hear my ancestors
speaking. my dripping fingers weave
gnarled amino acids, revealing
an ancient script — i was not intentional,

yet i'm here, following my tangled
roots. in india, archaeologists uncover
a rakhigarhi burial site, siphoning dna
from a four-thousand-year-old ear

bone, proving we south asians
descend from her
indus magic. grandma's gentle hands
don't arrive in the mail,

but she's listening
as am i.

interview as a portrait of fatherly intimacy

i am my father's child.
i know this

as sure as contraction
& expansion of my veins.

an intimate ribcage knowledge
i can't deny. his mother, my grandmother,

inhabits my bones, as does her mother.
their blood cemented in mine. at night,

i dream of her. she buries
wisdom under my skin. leaf-

letters i unfold
in the morning. i am

my father's child. i have never
met him. he has never seen me.

in a magazine interview, he's asked
about his family & his children. he

laughs, calls himself *a confirmed
bachelor*, but i breathe a sigh

of relief when he doesn't deny me,
doesn't say, i have no children.

in the same interview, he talks
of his mother. honey in his words.

he was his mother's child. her name is
Sayida. Sayida.

Sayida rolls off my tongue, pinches
my cheeks. she grew

up in kolkata, a student of rokeya
sakhawat hossain. like me, they

wanted liberation for women, for all.
who else breathed this into me?

i am my father's child. when asked
what he would be if not a filmmaker

he says, *writer.* and i know
i am my father's child. his imprint

stamped in the knotting of my joints,
in the vermilion of my platelets, in

the sand of my skin. i am my father's
child. i am my grandmother's spirit. i am

the bones i carry, a blossoming
of calcium & a lineage i cherish.

i am
Bengalee.

a prayer to my ancestors

bengalee ancestors, i call on you.

find you swimming in the rivers
of my bones. your spirits' wisdom
bathing in my marrow. i am

the west bengal muslim migrating
after the 1947 partition
of india. i am

the mukti bahini fighting
in the 1971 war for liberation. i am
the rickshaw my grandmother pulled,

rescuing hindi girls from
a war not of their making. i am
the lost languages, the lost

recipes across european-dictated
borders. i am the bird
flying over barbed wire, the smuggled

cow lifted by a crane
across the fence. i am the refugee,
craving a spot to call home. i am

the august floods, the monsoon rains,
the delta silt. bengalee ancestors,
what words can you gift me

to deepen the magic of your heritage?
amerikkka's falsified promises rage
against the peninsulas of my lungs,

sneaking a flag into my heart. i
pull it out, shred it, burn it. no flags
will take root in my body. i am

made of people, not nationalities.
Ancestors, we looked at the same sky,
conversed with the same moon. now,

i dream with you. i dream
of a world breathing free without
shackles, chains, & police knees.

Ancestors, you conjured
my body into being, protected me, held me
when no one else did. in your eyes,

the ones i see reflected in the mirror, i
see a future, not yet ready, waiting
to be born. & i hope i'm making

your dreams come true.

fill my bowl with a caesura salad

the crouton crunch of syllabics   my voice mimicking the sharp bite of parmesan

my origin also disputed   i am a royal romaine writer   a spring mix of words

like most origin stories   there are different versions of the same salad

    simple, yet profound—a few key ingredients   best used fresh

          if a salad was a story   what would it say?

FTP & fuck 12   the red sun glowing through a smoky fire   i am of my own making

a cumulus cloud tucked low in the sky   the wind pushing for rebellion   howling

ready to eat her whole?   i am a bee caught in the surface tension of a pool

    america & poland rust in my throat   bangla dangles in my lips, am i

        i am of three cultures   neither passed down to me

embracing my emotions   living my joy   scattering my pollen   birthing my many petals

i lust for words   slithering between ink   i am   a shapla water lily thriving

my beauty floats under my flesh   i am a book fiend   a book snake

of my chosen femininity   don't suggest i wax my eyebrows or my legs

don't call me a woman   call me a lover

*note: poem is to be read from the bowl's bottom to its top, because our foundations and our origins are what makes us, us. but it can also be read top to bottom if so chosen because this is your poem as much as it is mine.

digging up suicide

my feet submerged in dirt under-
neath fruit trees, my skin avoids
the sunlight flowing down
into my roots' sweet strength. soil
swallows me whole. i sink
down & down, picturing pink
pills spilling into my hand & sky
vodka burning my throat. i
picture slurps & gulps. i picture
soft silt hitting my cheeks. i float
through dappled brown
towards the unconscious.

my roots bellow —
open your eyes, face
your reflection, face
your mulch black irises,
see what i see — a seed
cracking open.

i repeat to myself —
i will survive. i will
survive.

i do not take the pills. i do not
chug the sky. i pull
weeds. i prune
branches. i allow the universe's
warmth to stroke clandestine
foliage. i rise from mother earth,
gazing up into a persimmon sunset,
a promise whisper falling
from my dirt-

dusted lips — i will see
tomorrow's peach sunrise.

breathe. breathe. breathe.

on some nights, i pour bourbon
down my throat hoping
for salvation that smells
like a grave. i've dug in the dirt,
found only worms eating
my core; i am seedless & sour.

on some nights, i pour bourbon
down my throat to soothe
my trauma response, where
loud sounds like heavy knocks
startle me. i'm afraid
when only three inches
separate me & whoever
is on the other side. i remember

child-me hiding under
the covers, teeth shaking as He
pounded on the door. in a dream,
i let Him in & slash His neck
with a razor, its sharp edges
biting His carotid artery.

in another dream, He calls me
pumpkin, sweetheart, baby
in His crooning voice. He
makes me feel wanted, loved,
seen with His mouth, His
fingers, His cock. i wake up,
gasping for breath, bile
rising in my throat, wishing
i could escape the forgotten
memories now falling like snow
on my breasts. it's too much,

this life, this body, this
flesh sack i carry, feeding
it, bathing it, sleeping it.
it never turns off, never
lets me be, a constant
memento of my abuse. i

breathe. & breathe. & breathe. &
breathe. until the invisible marks
He left on my body fade. until
each of my cells sings
the lullaby of oxygen. until

i don't pour bourbon
down my throat; my salvation
no longer found at the bottom
of a bottle; my salvation no longer
smelling like a grave, but
like the lavender i plant
in my garden. i dig

in the sky, find a rainbow, swallow
it whole & dance to the tune
of my healing, where ~~H~~he
no longer haunts my dreams
like a sick ghost, where i
am seedful & sweet.

forget everything that came after

remember the first time the sun held you
in its radiant embrace / how warm rays
touched your flesh / how solar flares

thundered in your breath / remember
the first time you placed your lips
on a nipple or a pacifier or a bottle / you

suckled, squeezed / soothing your body / you
gurgled, smiled. how possible you were /
a full moon rising / a redwood tree

expanding / a bird's wings kissing
the sky. remember how fresh the air
smelled / jasmine & honeysuckle / dawn

after rain / ocean at night. you didn't have
the words to say any of this / you'd only heard
a few voices — flour & gravel / or maybe

nothing at all. maybe you only sensed
the world around you with your skin, soaking up
the vibrations in your little toes. remember

what it was like to be born, pushed out
from the womb / slick in blood or maybe
you were lifted out / the womb cut open

to release you. remember your placenta /
how it linked you to another body / nourished
you selflessly / cared for you / asking

nothing in return / how it died after you

were expelled / how stroking your belly
button brings back these memories.

remember the unremembered — your first
breath lifting your lungs, tasting
your nostrils / when you had no idea

who you'd be or how you'd grow. the universe
splayed its energies / across light years &
birthed your soul. remember

you are a blessing & forget / everything
that came after.

the charred eyeless monster in the mirror

depression traps me under
the comfort of a heavy blanket —
neverending to-do lists itching

at my toes, clocks knocking at my knees,
self-threats curled around my throat.
depression eats my hunger, drinks

my thirst. what is hunger to a body at war
with you? what is water when my will
to live is akin to a flower's

in the middle of a los angeles drought?
depression infects my throat, my
sinuses, crumbles my immune system

like an ancient relic. it demands
i don't wash my face or brush
my teeth, don't take a shower or

change my pj's. depression ignites
my eyelids, crisps my lashes, burns
my brow. it waits for me

in the bathroom mirror — a charred eyeless
monster of melancholy. shrouded
in tiny thorns of capitalist neglect, ashes

of patriarchal memories searing its skin,
the monster growls. i am no longer
afraid, knowing its pain is my own.

i welcome it, let it tour my veins, ride
the ferris wheel of my ribs, visit
the islands of my marrow. i treat it

with kindness & cotton candy. it'll tire
& when it does, i'll take a breath
& exhale its gnawing anguish.

it'll go home & i'll still be here,
more alive than i thought possible.

learning to pick up the pieces

a glass cup slips through my fingers,
fireworks across the night sky
of the linoleum tiled kitchen floor.

a shattered mind disappearing
under or behind the fridge.
i have forgotten who i am. forgotten

how to see myself. my pillow is a
best friend, my blanket is a lover,
& my bed is a family holding my sobs.

today, i am fractured, without
the strength to pick up my pieces.
tomorrow, i will check under

the fridge, not prick my fingers
on the sadness lurking in corners.
tomorrow, i will breathe without

choking, i will fall without breaking.
i won't be glass. i will be
a whole cup / brimming with me.

self-growth

an arachnid swings
on her web / her six eyes

observe me rinsing
my coffee cup / her eight legs,

thin & long, perch
on silver streaks / for weeks,

we are companions / then
she's gone / hiding behind

the kitchen cabinet / shedding
her shell / unmasking her

soft pulp / soon, she'll emerge
bigger / hardened / her vulnerability

embraced / she'll reconstruct
her silk strands / catch her prey

confident & brave / never forgetting
her tender survival /

i touch trees & feel rooted

i wasn't born,
bark & branch.

at night, i stumble
awake into a hollow

trunk. shadows gasping
at my dark. i wasn't

born, bark & branch.
i grow roots. an owl

hoots, calls me home.
i echo.

an ode to my feathered friends

what is it about birds

                that makes me feel

                                like i can fly too?

their wings

                eat the sky. their beaks

                        nibble on clouds. they swallow

        trees with their songs. their talons

                    imbibe omens for the sharp swelling

of freedom. what is it about birds

                that makes me feel

                          like i can fly too?

they consume thousands

                        of blue miles under

            their feathers & never look back. they gnaw

        waves with their webbed feet,

                      let the current do the rest.

a pecky confidence i envy.

                          they build homes from scraps they find.

yes, it is birds

                who remind me wings

                          devour my spine & i can fly, too,

if i let go

                of the burdens in my belly

                          weighing me down.

portrait of potatoes as depression

today is ten pounds of potatoes
sitting on my chest. i smell
the dirt on their skins. the dirt

their birthplace, their origin
story. i lay under the covers,
imagining i am a potato,
safe in the earth. i am afraid

to live my truth. i am afraid
i'll be left to soften & rot
on the kitchen counter. loneliness

digs into me, hungry for my flesh,
as i hunger for warm fingers
on my spine. ten pounds of cold potatoes
swaddling my breasts. their sprouting

eyes staring at me, daring me to rise
& practice re-birth. we reproduce,
we replicate. we try to self-improve,

but we are trapped in cycles of sleep
& awake, where we repeat
the same patterns. i palm
the surface of a potato — dry

& bumpy like my mental health.
no matter how many affirmations
i speak, i return to this empty cellar.

i miss the thrill of a crush — how
once this was my antidote

to depression. a reason to fling
the potatoes off my chest. i want

a stranger's skin on mine
so i don't have to feel my own.
i'm tired of relying on others'

desires to keep me alive.
i stick out my tongue,
lick a potato, murmur
i love you. today i choose

to cherish what i dig out
from the ground. today,
i honor my dirt

& all that comes with it,
love myself & the ten
pounds of potatoes
sitting on my chest.

dear dawn,

you birth blushing petals, pollinated
with possibility, splayed across
a tender sky of baby blue. you bloom
into a day — a fierce flower flinging

bouquets into my hemisphere. you are
amber nectar hanging on my lips, whispering
a prayer in a language my tongue
remembers the way it remembers

the taste of tawny leaves. tomorrow, dawn,
you will germinate, again. outside, my dead
marigold buries its seeds, from its death
new life springs forth — a resurrection

planted in wilted endings & beginnings,
awaiting its rooted re-birth.

a day of joy

my alarm rings. i don't hit
snooze. i kiss the rising
sun on the lips, no depression
tugging at my hips,
begging me to stay in bed. some days,

i wish to snooze my life, hit the pause
button, sleep away the sorrow. not
today. today, i stand outside,
arms cradling the sky. the ghost
of my embodied aches finds
the staircase to a paradise,
floats away. i hope this fire
in my veins lasts forever. i know
it won't. today is enough.

i am a balloon,   weightless & free,
gliding up   up   up   up to make love to the sun.

a tulip plucked without consent

1.
a red tulip caged in a vase,
its final petal ready
to drop. a six year old
child falls asleep, dreams
of six petals wrapped
around her — arms
of her mother, of her
father, of her sister.

2.
years later, she awakens, sees
no petals on the tulip. the wails
of the stamen & pistil swirl
into her hair. she can't
get it out of her head. she can't
get out of bed. she lies there,
muffled in the pillow.

the tulip plucked
without consent, left
to die, severed
from her family.

3.
years later, she re-opens
her eyes, finding she is
not a corpse on display. she is
not unpetaled & alone. she lives,
she breathes, she fleshes. she is
here.

4.
years later, slowly,
she re-attaches
petals, choosing the colors,
re-claiming herself
one petal, one page
at a time.

ways to be a flower

listen to the sun. her rays
are stars of wisdom. they'll
teach you how to grow.

let snails & caterpillars nibble
your leaves. share yourself.
don't poison those who seek

your refuge. if a human picks you
wilt. they don't deserve your beauty
if they take you without asking.

sing to the bees. they'll feed
& spread your seed. give
but don't hesitate to receive.

root yourself. speak to soil.
express your needs. you are
important. you are enough.

let the wind blow away
your insecurities. don't
forget. bloom bright.

your time is brief.

acknowledgments

Writing a book is a gift to yourself and to others. It can't be done alone. Even during a pandemic.

I'd like to thank my Community Literature Initiative (CLI) Saturday Church. My cohort (Christiana, Christian, Lolo, Daniel, B.T., Anne Marie, Laurie, Evan, Jasmine, Tessa, Brenda, Diosa, and Adanna) kept me writing. A special thanks to my teachers, Tommy Domino and Ravina Wadhwani. As well as all our guest poets. And of course all the appreciation for Hiram Sims, who founded CLI and encouraged me to apply.

I would have never signed up for CLI if it hadn't been for Alex Petunia. Thank you for pushing me and encouraging me to share my story and for hosting monthly meditation sessions to keep us grounded in our poetry.

A big hug and shout-out to Los Angeles Poet Society (LAPS), especially Jessica M. Wilson — despite being socially distanced, LAPS kept me connected to my poetic community.

Super happy to have connected with Ayaskala Magazine, a mental health-focused literary journal based in India. Several of the poems in this collection were inspired by their April 2020 Poetry Month prompts.

Eternally appreciative to Alex Petunia and Vero for their last-minute feedback on a few poems.

Enormously grateful to World Stage Press for picking up my book. It was my dream press and I couldn't be happier to have my words published by them. Thank you, Krystle May Statler and Sara Khayat for kicking ass. Y'all are the best. Special mention, of course, to Emily Anne Evans from the CLI book design team for the initial interior layout.

Hugs and love to Ingrid M. Calderon-Collins for inspiring me to write and share my raw truth. You're a bad-ass.

This book was a lot for me. I don't think I would have been able to write it if I hadn't published my chapbook, *gathering grandmothers' bones*. A huge thank you to DSTL Arts and especially Luis Antonio Pichardo for always believing in me.

Thank you to the folks who came through to the Loop, a feedback session for poets, and provided me with invaluable critique, especially Kundan, Imogen, Brenda, Vero, Kiana, and Mauricio.

Filled with gratitude for connecting with Time to Tell, the 2021 Survivor Voices Showcase, Donna Jenson, and the Mod Squad — Beth and Maggie. Our retreat gave me the courage to embrace myself as a survivor. Without their support and love, some of these poems may have never ended up in this book.

A big hug to Nikolai Garcia who always supports me and my poetry. I appreciate you so much, friend.

And many more hugs to the rest of my poet-friends and my comrade-friends. I love you all. You are my family. Special shout-out to the b*ch krewe.

Lastly, I'd like to thank myself for having the courage to write and publish *loving my salt-drenched bones*.

Before being gathered into this collection, some of my poems found homes here:

> *my mother says everyone has to learn how to swim*, *song of my womb*, and *i can't love like a wild animal* appeared in Sixfold Journal

an ode to other mothers, *but you speak english so well*, and *a tulip plucked without consent* appeared in *María's at Sampaguitas*

on the gold line metro station stop appeared in *Sobotka Literary Magazine*

back to the past and *i don't have any dietary restrictions* appeared in *Ayaskala Magazine*

we find homes appeared in the *Altadena Poetry Review*

3.5 x 2 inch hugs, *english is not my language* and *grandma's hands* were previously published in my chapbook, *gathering grandmothers' bones*

english is not my language first appeared in *tenderness lit*

grandma's hands was also published by *Whoa Nelly Press*

fire to the prisons and *fill my bowl with a caesura salad* appeared in the *DSTL Art's Conchas y Café zines*

my non-binary femmefesto appeared in *Acid Verse Literary Journal* (under a different name)

rumination on menstruation appeared in *Resurrection Magazine*

breathe. breathe. breathe appeared in *Time to Tell's Survivor Voices: Original Works of Resilience Written by Survivors of Childhood Sexual Abuse*

healing isn't chronological appeared in *Beneath the Soil*, an e-zine by and for survivors

a map of my mother's pain, *days like this i don't want to live*, and *a prayer to my ancestors* appeared in *Cultural Daily*

about the author

karo ska (she/they) is a South Asian & Eastern European non-binary femme poet, living on unceded Tongva Land. They migrated here in 1996 from Warsaw, Poland. Anti-capitalist & anti-authoritarian, they find joy where they can. Some of their other work appears in *Dryland Lit, Resurrection Magazine, the Intercultural Press, Altadena Poetry Review, Cultural Daily, Marías at Sampaguitas,* and *Ayaskala Magazine.* They are a 3-time 2020 Pushcart Prize nominee and were a semi-finalist in the Jack Grapes Poetry Prize. Their first chapbook, *gathering grandmothers' bones* was released on February 29th, 2020. For updates, follow them on instagram @ karoo_skaa or check out their website karoska.com.

www.ingramcontent.com/pod-product-compliance
Lightning Source LLC
Chambersburg PA
CBHW031322160426
43196CB00007B/620